Envision It! | Visual Skills Handbook

Cause and Effect

Main Idea and Details

Literary Elements

Cause and Effect

Cause   Effect

Main Idea and Details

Main Idea

Details

Literary Elements

Characters

DADDY
MOMMY
BROTHER
SISTER

Setting

Plot

Beginning

Middle

End

Envision It! | Visual Strategies Handbook

Background Knowledge

Important Ideas

Inferring

Monitor and Clarify

Predict and Set Purpose

Questioning

Story Structure

Summarize

Text Structure

Visualize

Background Knowledge

Let's Think About Reading!

- What do I already know?
- What does this remind me of?

Important Ideas

Let's **Think** About **Reading!**

- What is important to know?

Inferring

Let's Think About Reading!

- What do I already know?
- How does this help me understand what happened?

Monitor and Clarify

Let's **Think** About **Reading!**

- What does not make sense?
- How can I fix it?

Predict and Set Purpose

Trains

Let's Think About Reading!

- What do I already know?
- What do I think will happen?
- What is my purpose for reading?

Questioning

Let's Think About Reading!

- What questions do I have about what I am reading?

Story Structure

Beginning

Middle

End

Let's Think About Reading!

- What happens in the beginning?
- What happens in the middle?
- What happens in the end?

Summarize

The dog knocked over the table.

Let's Think About Reading!

- What happens in the story?
- What is the story mainly about?

Text Structure

Let's **Think** About **Reading!**

- How is the story organized?
- Are there any patterns?

Visualize

SCOTT FORESMAN
READING STREET

GRADE 1

COMMON CORE ©

Program Authors

Peter Afflerbach

Camille Blachowicz

Candy Dawson Boyd

Elena Izquierdo

Connie Juel

Edward Kame'enui

Donald Leu

Jeanne R. Paratore

P. David Pearson

Sam Sebesta

Deborah Simmons

Susan Watts Taffe

Alfred Tatum

Sharon Vaughn

Karen Kring Wixson

Glenview, Illinois

Boston, Massachusetts

Chandler, Arizona

Upper Saddle River, New Jersey

ALWAYS LEARNING

PEARSON

We dedicate *Reading Street* to
Peter Jovanovich.

His wisdom, courage,
and passion for education
are an inspiration to us all.

Acknowledgments appear on page 188, which constitutes an extension of this copyright page.

ISBN-13: 978-0-328-72444-4
ISBN-10: 0-328-72444-0
3 4 5 6 7 8 9 10 V063 16 15 14 13 12

Dear Reader,

How is your trip along *Scott Foresman Reading Street* so far? Have you enjoyed meeting all the characters?

As you go a little farther down *Reading Street*, you will meet more exciting characters, such as a pig in a wig, a blue ox, and a fox and a kit.

You will be reading articles and stories about tame animals and wild ones. And your reading will be getting better and better along the way!

Sincerely,
The Authors

Unit 1 Contents

Animals, Tame and Wild

How are people and animals important to one another?

Week 2

Week 3

Unit 1 Contents

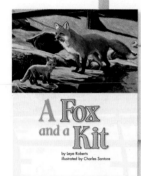

Week 6

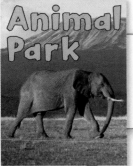

Envision It! A Comprehension Handbook

**Envision It! Visual Skills
Handbook EI•1–EI•5**

**Envision It! Visual Strategies
Handbook EI•7–EI•17**

READING STREET The Digital Path!

Don Leu
The Internet Guy

Right before our eyes, the nature of reading and learning is changing. The Internet and other technologies create new opportunities, new solutions, and new literacies. New reading comprehension skills are required online. They are increasingly important to our students and our society.

Those of us on the Reading Street team are here to help you on this new, and very exciting, journey.

See It!

- Big Question Video

- Concept Talk Video

- Envision It! Animations

- eReaders

- Interactive Sound-Spelling Cards

bread

ea

Hear It!

- *Sing with Me Animations*

- eSelections

- Grammar Jammer

- Vocabulary Activities

pronouns

I, me, he, she, they, we

Concept Talk Video

File   Edit   View   Favorites   Tools   Help

http://www.ReadingStreet.com

Do It!

- **Journal Word Bank**

- **Story Sort**

- **Letter Tile Drag and Drop**

- **Online Assessment**

- **Vocabulary Activities**

Animals, Tame and Wild

THE BIG ?

How are people and animals important to one another?

10

Common Core State Standards

Speaking/Listening 4. Describe people, places, things, and events with relevant details, expressing ideas and feelings clearly. **Also Language 5.c.**

Let's Talk About

Read Together

Animal Friends

- Share information about pets and other tame animals.
- Discuss the needs of pets.

READING STREET ONLINE
CONCEPT TALK VIDEO
www.ReadingStreet.com

13

Common Core State Standards

Foundational Skills 2.c. Isolate and pronounce initial, medial vowel, and final sounds (phonemes) in spoken single-syllable words. **Also Foundational Skills 2.a., 2.b.**

Let's Listen for

Sounds

- Find five things that contain the short *a* sound.
- Find five things that end with the sound /k/.
- Find something that rhymes with *luck*. Say each sound in the word.
- Find two things that rhyme with *pant*.

READING STREET ONLINE
SOUND-SPELLING CARDS
www.ReadingStreet.com

Read Together

COME IN

14

Common Core State Standards
Foundational Skills 3. Know and apply grade-level phonics and word analysis skills in decoding words.
Also Foundational Skills 3.g.

Envision It! | Sounds to Know

astronaut

short a

READING STREET ONLINE
SOUND-SPELLING CARDS
www.ReadingStreet.com

Phonics

Short *a: a*

Words I Can Blend

P	a	t
c	a	n
t	a	g
D	a	d
s	a	t

Sentences I Can Read

1. Pat can tag me.

2. Dad sat.

Words I Can Read

| my |
| come |
| way |
| on |
| in |

Sentences I Can Read

1. Sam can nap on my lap.

2. Dan can come in that way, Matt.

Common Core State Standards
Foundational Skills 3.a. Know the
spelling-sound correspondences for
common consonant digraphs.
Also Foundational Skills 3., 3.g.

Phonics

🔊 Consonant Pattern -ck

Words I Can Blend

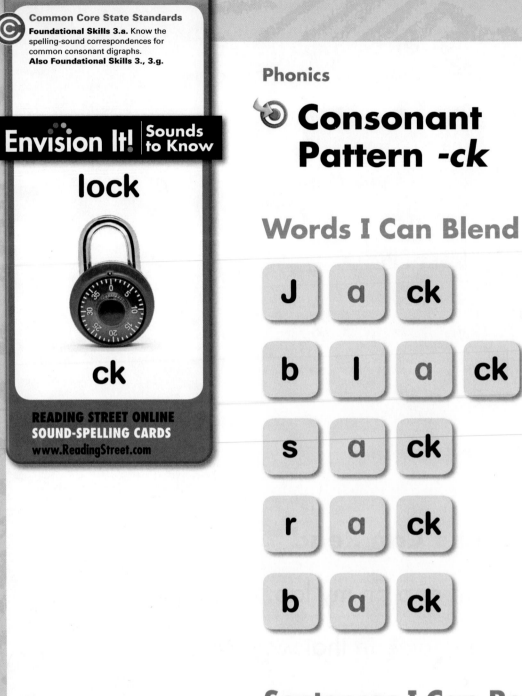

J a ck

b l a ck

s a ck

r a ck

b a ck

Sentences I Can Read

1. Hand Jack a black sack.

2. Can Dan nab that back rack?

Common Core State Standards
Foundational Skills 3.a. Know the
spelling-sound correspondences for
common consonant digraphs.

I Can Read!

"I am Ann, an ant." Ann sat on a plant that my pal Jack Cat had.

Jack Cat ran in to pack for camp. "Can an ant come, Jack?" Can Jack Cat ask Dad?

Jack can ask Dad. "Pack Ann Ant! Ann Ant can camp!"

"Camp! Way to go, Jack!"

You've learned

- Short *a*: *a*
- Consonant Pattern *-ck*

High-Frequency Words

my   come   way   on   in

Sam, Come Back!

by Susan Stevens Crummel
illustrated by Janet Stevens

 **Genre**

Realistic fiction tells about made-up events that could happen in real life. Next you will read about Sam and Jack, who are made-up characters.

 Question of the Week

What do pets need?

Sam the cat is on my lap.

Sam ran. Sam, come back!

Sam ran that way.
Nab that cat!

See Sam in the sack.

Sam ran that way.
Nab that cat!

See Sam in the pack.

Bad Sam! Sam, come back!

Jack, Jack! Sam is back.
Pat Sam on my lap.

Common Core State Standards
Literature 1. Ask and answer questions about key details in a text.
Also Literature 2., Writing 5.

Think Critically

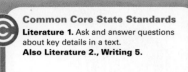

1. What part of the story do you think is funny? Why? Text to Self

2. Why do you think the author wrote this story? Author's Purpose

3. Where does Sam run? Why do you think he runs there?

   Character and Setting

4. Reread page 24. If you did not know what the word *nab* means, what could you do to figure it out?

   Monitor and Clarify

5. **Look Back and Write** Look back at page 25. Where does Sam run first? Write about it.

   Key Ideas and Details • Text Evidence

READING STREET ONLINE
STORY SORT
www.ReadingStreet.com

30

Susan Stevens Crummel

Susan Stevens Crummel loves all animals. Her cat, Tweeter, likes to sit in the chair by the computer.

Ms. Crummel wrote poems and songs when she was a child. She even wrote skits for her sister Janet to act out for friends.

Here are other books by Susan Stevens Crummel.

Use the Reading Log in the *Reader's and Writer's Notebook* to record your independent reading.

31

Common Core State Standards

Language 2. Demonstrate command of the conventions of standard English capitalization, punctuation, and spelling when writing. **Also Writing 5., Language 2.b.**

Let's Write It!

Read Together

Key Features of a Story

- has characters and tells what they do
- is made of sentences

**READING STREET ONLINE
GRAMMAR JAMMER
www.ReadingStreet.com**

Story

A **story** tells about characters. It tells what they do. The student model on the next page is an example of a story.

Writing Prompt Think about a pet you know. Write a story about the pet playing.

Writer's Checklist

Remember, you should . . .

- ☑ tell the kind of pet and what it does.
- ☑ show how you feel about the pet.
- ☑ begin each sentence with an uppercase, or capital, letter and end it with a period.

My Dog Rex

Rex has a toy duck.

He plays with it.

He puts it in his bed.

Rex is my best friend.

Sentences tell complete ideas. They begin with capital letters and end with periods.

Genre Story
The character is a dog named Rex.

Writing Trait Voice
The last sentence shows how the writer feels.

Conventions

● **Sentences**

Remember A **sentence** is a group of words that tells a complete idea. Say the sentence about the dog. **The dog is big.**

Common Core State Standards
Literature 10. With prompting and support, read prose and poetry of appropriate complexity for grade 1.

Genre
Sing-Along

- A sing-along is a song people sing together. Sometimes new words are sung to an old tune.

- A sing-along is a poem set to music. It has rhythm, or a regular pattern of beats.

- Some lines in a sing-along may repeat. Some words may rhyme.

- As you read "Puppy Games," think about what makes it a sing-along.

Read Together

Sing to the tune of "Frère Jacques."

Puppy Games

by Linda Lott
illustrated by Maribel Suarez

Yap! Come play now!
Yap! Come play now!
Let's have fun.
Let's have fun.

I can tug on your socks.
I'll knock over your blocks.
Then I'll nap
In your lap.

Let's **Think** About...

What words in this sing-along rhyme? What is the sing-along's rhythm? Clap your hands to show it.
Sing-Along

Let's **Think** About...

Reading Across Texts How do the owners of Sam in *Sam, Come Back!* and the owner of the puppy in "Puppy Games" feel about their pets' actions?

Writing Across Texts Write sentences about what the puppy in the sing-along and Sam do. Use rhythm and rhyme.

Common Core State Standards
Speaking/Listening 1.c. Ask questions to clear up any confusion about the topics and texts under discussion. **Also Foundational Skills 4.**

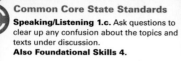

Let's **Learn** It!

Read Together

READING STREET ONLINE
VOCABULARY ACTIVITIES
www.ReadingStreet.com

Listening and Speaking

Get Ready For Grade 2

Ask a speaker questions if you don't understand something.

Ask Questions When someone is speaking, we listen carefully. If we do not understand something, we wait until the speaker is finished. Then we ask questions.

Practice It! Ask a partner to tell you about what pets need. Listen carefully. Ask questions to make sure you understand. Then tell your partner about what a pet needs. When your partner asks you questions, listen carefully to each one so that you know exactly what your partner is asking. Then answer the questions.

Vocabulary

Location words tell where things are.

a cat **over** a mat   a cat **under** a mat

Practice It! Read these words. Use each word to tell where something is.

on   up   in   out

Fluency

Accuracy When you read, try to read with no mistakes.

Practice It!

1. Sam can come back.

2. Jack can snap the pack.

3. The black cat sat.

Common Core State Standards

Speaking/Listening 4. Describe people, places, things, and events with relevant details, expressing ideas and feelings clearly. **Also Speaking/Listening 1.**

Oral Vocabulary

Let's Talk About

Animal Friends

- Share ideas about how people help animals.

- Discuss the kinds of jobs there are in which people help animals.

Phonemic Awareness

Let's Listen for

Sounds

- Find five things that contain the short *i* sound in the middle of the word.

- Find something that has the short *i* sound at the beginning of the word. Say the word.

- Find four things that rhyme with *sick*. Say each word.

- Find something that rhymes with *six*. Say the sound at the end of that word.

- Find something that rhymes with *wish*. Say each sound in the word.

Read Together

READING STREET ONLINE
SOUND-SPELLING CARDS
www.ReadingStreet.com

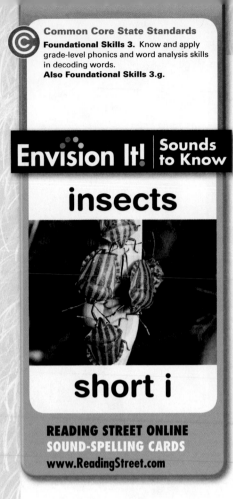

Envision It! | Sounds to Know

insects

short i

READING STREET ONLINE
SOUND-SPELLING CARDS
www.ReadingStreet.com

Phonics

Short *i: i*

Words I Can Blend

w i l l

p i ck

t r i ck

d i d

b i g

Sentences I Can Read

1. Dad will pick that trick.

2. Did that big bag sag?

Words I Can Read

she

take

what

up

Sentences I Can Read

1. She will take it back.

2. What did Bill pick up?

Envision It! | **Sounds to Know**

fox

x

Phonics

🔊 Consonant x/ks/

Words I Can Blend

M	a	x
f	i	x
s	a	x
m	i	x
s	i	x

Sentences I Can Read

1. Max will fix the sax.

2. Mix it at six.

What can Nick fix? Quick, Nick! Fix the grill. Max can pick it up and take it with him.

Will Trix fix ham? She can fix it on the grill for Bill. It will fill him up.

Max will sit and sip milk. Milk will fill him up.

You've learned

- Short *i: i*
- Consonant x/ks/

High-Frequency Words
she   take   what   up

Pig in a Wig

by Susan Stevens Crummel
illustrated by Janet Stevens

 **Genre**

An **animal fantasy** is a story about animals that could not really happen. In the next story, you will read about a pig that does things a real pig cannot do.

 Read Together

Who helps animals?

Pig in a wig is big, you see.

Tick, tick, tick.
It is three.

Pig can mix.
Mix it up.

Pig can dip.
Dip it up.

Pig can lick.
Lick it up.

It is six. Tick, tick, tick.
Pig is sad. She is sick.

Fix that pig.
Take a sip.

Fix that pig.
Quick, quick, quick!

Max, Max! Take the sax!
Play it, Max, and play it, Pam!

Pig in a wig did a jig.
What a ham!

Common Core State Standards

Literature 1. Ask and answer questions about key details in a text. **Also Literature 2., 9., Writing 5.**

Think Critically

1. How is Pig like Sam in *Sam, Come Back!?* Text to Text

2. How does the author make Pig seem silly? Think Like an Author

3. What problem does Pig have? How does Pig solve the problem? Plot

4. Tell about the important events in the story. Summarize

5. **Look Back and Write** Look back at page 57. How does Pig feel? Write about it. Use evidence from the story.

   Key Ideas and Details • Text Evidence

Janet Stevens

Janet Stevens always wanted to draw pictures. She enjoys drawing pictures for children's books.

Ms. Stevens practices drawing all the time. "Practice helps a lot in whatever you try to do," she says. She likes to draw pigs, cats, and bears.

Here are other books illustrated by Janet Stevens.

Use the Reading Log in the *Reader's and Writer's Notebook* to record your independent reading.

Common Core State Standards

Writing 3. Write narratives in which they recount two or more appropriately sequenced events, include some details regarding what happened, use temporal words to signal event order, and provide some sense of closure. **Also Speaking/Listening 5., Language 1., 2.**

Let's Write It!

Read Together

Key Features of a Fantasy Story

- characters and events are made up
- characters do things that real people and animals cannot do

READING STREET ONLINE
GRAMMAR JAMMER
www.ReadingStreet.com

Fantasy Story

A **fantasy story** has events that cannot really happen. The student model on the next page is an example of a fantasy story.

Writing Prompt Write a fantasy story about a person who helps an animal. Draw a picture for your story.

Writer's Checklist

Remember, you should . . .

☑ use your imagination to write and draw a picture.

☑ begin each sentence with a capital letter and end it with a period.

☑ make sure each sentence has a subject.

The Pet Cow

Bob has a pet cow.

Cow likes to cook.

It makes a big mess.

Bob gives Cow a bath.

Each sentence has a **subject.**

Writing Trait Conventions
Sentences begin with capital letters and end with periods.

Genre Fantasy Story
A real cow cannot cook.

Conventions

● **Subjects of Sentences**

Remember A sentence has a
● **subject,** or naming part.

The pig did a jig.

Common Core State Standards
Literature 10. With prompting and support, read prose and poetry of appropriate complexity for grade 1.

Social Studies in Reading

Genre
Sing-Along

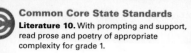
Read Together

- A song people sing together is sometimes called a sing-along. New words may be sung to a well-known tune.

- A sing-along is a poem set to music. It has clear rhythm, and some of the words may rhyme.

- Kids might sing a sing-along during a long car ride with their families or at summer camp with other kids.

- Read "We Are Vets." As you read, look for elements that make it a sing-along.

We Are Vets

by Linda Lott
illustrated by Lindsey Gardiner

Sing to the tune of "Three Blind Mice."

We are vets.

We are vets.

We help pets.

We help pets.

If you have a dog who is feeling sick,

Bring him to me, and I'll fix him quick.

His tail will wag, and he'll chase a stick.

He'll feel fine. He'll feel fine.

Let's Think About...

Which words rhyme in this sing-along? What is its rhythm?
Sing-Along

Let's Think About...

Reading Across Texts The pig in *Pig in a Wig* and the dog in "We Are Vets" both feel sick. Who helps them get better? How?

Writing Across Texts Write a poem about what the two animals do after they get better. Use rhythm and rhyme in your poem.

Common Core State Standards
Speaking/Listening 1. Participate in collaborative conversations about grade 1 topics and texts with peers and adults in small and larger groups. **Also Foundational Skills 4.b., Speaking/Listening 1.a.**

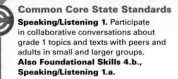

Let's **Learn** It!

Read Together

READING STREET ONLINE VOCABULARY ACTIVITIES
www.ReadingStreet.com

> I have a cat named Button. I feed him and give him fresh water every day. I brush him so his fur is shiny and clean. He likes that.

Get Ready For Grade 2

Listen carefully when others are speaking.

Listening and Speaking

Share Information and Ideas When we tell others our ideas, we speak clearly so that they understand us. When others tell us their ideas, we listen so that we understand them.

Practice It! When asked, tell others how you care for an animal. Then let them tell you how they care for an animal. Follow the rules. Listen carefully. Take notes to help you understand.

Vocabulary

These words are in **alphabetical order.** Look at the first letter in each word. Think about the alphabet.

ant

bat

cat

Practice It! Read these words. Write them in alphabetical order.

big   **dip**   **am**   **can**

Fluency

Accuracy When you read, try to read with no mistakes.

Practice It!

1. Max can mix it.

2. The black cat licks Bill.

3. She will take the sack.

Common Core State Standards

Speaking/Listening 1. Participate in collaborative conversations about grade 1 topics and texts with peers and adults in small and larger groups.
Also Language 5.c.

Let's Talk About

Read Together

Animal Friends

- Contribute to a discussion about the kinds of animals that help people.

- Share information about how animals help people.

READING STREET ONLINE
CONCEPT TALK VIDEO
www.ReadingStreet.com

67

Common Core State Standards
Foundational Skills 2.c. Isolate and pronounce initial, medial vowel, and final sounds (phonemes) in spoken single-syllable words. **Also Foundational Skills 2., 2.b.**

Let's Listen for

Sounds

- Find five things that have the short *o* sound in the middle.

- Find something that has the short *o* sound at the beginning of the word. Say the word.

- Find two things that rhyme with *stop*. Say each word.

- Find something that rhymes with *pot*. Say the sound at the end of that word.

- Find something that rhymes with *rows*. Say each sound in the word.

READING STREET ONLINE
SOUND-SPELLING CARDS
www.ReadingStreet.com

Read Together

Common Core State Standards
Foundational Skills 3. Know and apply grade-level phonics and word analysis skills in decoding words.
Also Foundational Skills 3.b., 3.g.

Envision It! | Sounds to Know

octopus

short o

READING STREET ONLINE
SOUND-SPELLING CARDS
www.ReadingStreet.com

Phonics

Short *o*: *o*

Words I Can Blend

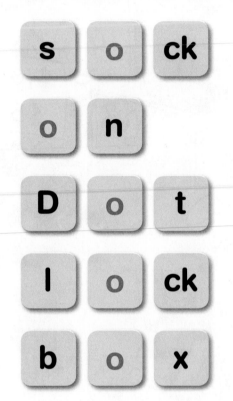

s o ck

o n

D o t

l o ck

b o x

Sentences I Can Read

1. Jan can fit that sock on Dot.

2. Lock that big box.

Words I Can Read

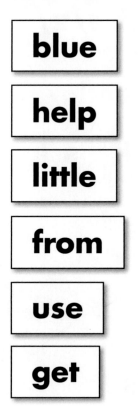

blue

help

little

from

use

get

Sentences I Can Read

1. Help him fix the little blue clock.

2. Get the mop from Jon and use it.

Common Core State Standards

Foundational Skills 3. Know and apply grade-level phonics and word analysis skills in decoding words.
Also Foundational Skills 3.b., 3.g.

Phonics

Plural -s, Consonant s/z/

Words I Can Blend

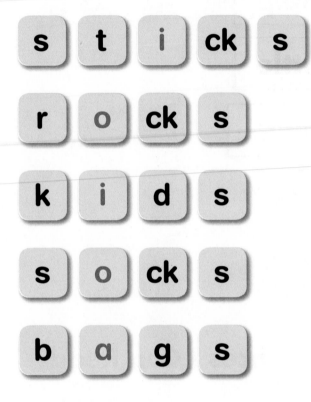

s t i ck s

r o ck s

k i d s

s o ck s

b a g s

Sentences I Can Read

1. Mom will grab sticks and rocks.

2. Kids can drop socks in bags.

I Can Read!

Tom is on my block. His job is to help little kids get help from big kids. Lots of kids can use help.

Kip can spot his blue block drop in Fox Pond. Rob and Tom got it.

Wags can drag socks in the sand. Rob and Tom will stop that. Rob and Tom did big jobs.

The Big Blue Ox

by Susan Stevens Crummel

illustrated by Janet Stevens

Genre

An **animal fantasy** is a make-believe story with animals that act like people. Next you will read about an ox that acts like a person. What do you want to find out? Set a purpose for reading.

Read Together

How do animals help people?

75

Mom and Pop have a big blue ox.

Ox can help. He is big.
He can pick, and he can dig.

Pigs in wigs sit in mud.
Ox can help a little!

Get the mop from Mom and Pop.
Mop the pigs. Fix the wigs.

Off to town go Mom and Pop.
Ox can help! Hop on top.

Get the cans. Pack the sack.
Ox can help! Take it back.

Ox can help! Use big pans.
He is hot. Use big fans!

Mom and Pop nap on Ox.
Ox is a big, big help.

Common Core State Standards
Literature 1. Ask and answer questions about key details in a text.
Also Literature 2., Writing 5.

Envision It! Retell

READING STREET ONLINE
STORY SORT
www.ReadingStreet.com

84

Think Critically

1. Ox is a helpful friend. How do you help your friends and family? Text to Self

2. Why do you think the author decided Ox would be big? Author's Purpose

3. Who are the characters in this story? Where does this story take place?

   Character and Setting

4. What pictures did you see in your mind of Ox helping?

   Visualize

5. Look Back and Write Look back at pages 79–82. Write some things Ox can do to help. Be sure to use evidence from the story.

   Key Ideas and Details • Text Evidence

Susan Stevens Crummel and Janet Stevens

Susan Stevens Crummel and Janet Stevens are sisters! They have fun working together. Ms. Crummel writes down ideas and turns them into a story. She sends the story to her sister Janet, who draws pictures to fit the story.

Here are other books written and illustrated by Susan Stevens Crummel and Janet Stevens.

COOK-A-DOODLE-DOO!
Janet Stevens and Susan Stevens Crummel

JANET STEVENS AND SUSAN STEVENS CRUMMEL
And the DISH Ran Away with the SPOON

Reading Log

Use the Reading Log in the *Reader's and Writer's Notebook* to record your independent reading.

Common Core State Standards
Language 1.j. Produce and expand complete simple and compound declarative, interrogative, imperative, and exclamatory sentences in response to prompts. **Also Writing 5.**

Let's Write It!

Read Together

Key Features of a Short Poem

- has words written in lines that may rhyme
- can describe something or can express feelings

READING STREET ONLINE
GRAMMAR JAMMER
www.ReadingStreet.com

Short Poem

A **short poem** has words written in lines. In many poems, the lines rhyme. The student model on the next page shows two examples of short poems.

Writing Prompt Think about a kind of animal you know. Write a two-line poem about that animal.

Writer's Checklist

Remember, you should . . .

☑ write a poem two lines long about a kind of animal.

☑ make the lines rhyme if you wish. Say the sentences.

☑ make sure each sentence you say has a predicate.

A Fast Cat

Can a cat run up a hill?
Yes, yes, a fast cat will.

A Hen

A hen ran up to the men.
A man fed corn to the hen.

A sentence tells
a complete idea.

The **predicate**
of the sentence
tells what
someone does.

**Genre
Short Poem**
Read a **poem**
aloud. In the
sentences, words
that rhyme
sound alike.

Conventions

● **Predicates of Sentences**

Remember A sentence has a
predicate, a telling part. It tells what a
person or thing does. Say the sentences.

Ox **helps Mom and Pop.** He **sits.**

Common Core State Standards

Informational Text 5. Know and use various text features (e.g., headings, tables of contents, glossaries, electronic menus, icons) to locate key facts or information in a text. **Also Informational Text 6., 7.**

Genre

Photo Essay

Read Together

- A photo essay is made up of photographs and words about one topic. The photographs help readers understand the words.

- Photographs can help readers connect with real people, places, and events.

- The photographs in a photo essay are usually displayed on the pages in a creative way.

- As you read "They Can Help," think about what makes it a photo essay.

They Can Help

by Pat Waris

We can use help.
Can we get help?

Let's **Think** About...

Would the words on these pages make sense without the photographs? Why or why not?
Photo Essay

The big dog can help.

The little dog can help.

89

Let's **Think** About...

How do these photographs show what the words are telling?
Photo Essay

Let's **Think** About...

Retell the order of events in the text using the words.
Photo Essay

The big dog can help.

The little dog can help.

90

In what ways do they help?

Let's **Think** About...

How do these photographs answer the question on the page? **Photo Essay**

Let's **Think** About...

Reading Across Texts How are Ox in *The Big Blue Ox* and the animals in "They Can Help" different? How are the ways they help people different?

Writing Across Texts Draw pictures of Ox helping and an animal in the photo essay helping. Write sentences that tell what they are doing.

Common Core State Standards
Speaking/Listening 4. Describe people, places, things, and events with relevant details, expressing ideas and feelings clearly. **Also Foundational Skills 4.**

Micah, this is Sara. Sara is in my class. She likes to play soccer just like you!

Let's Learn It!

Read Together

**READING STREET ONLINE
VOCABULARY ACTIVITIES**
www.ReadingStreet.com

Get Ready For Grade 2

Speak clearly when introducing people.

Listening and Speaking

Give Introductions When we introduce someone to someone else, we say both of their names. We tell something about the two people. We make sure to speak clearly.

Practice It! Practice introducing friends. Say both of their names clearly. Remember something you know about your friends and tell it to them.

Vocabulary

A **synonym** is a word that means the same or almost the same thing as another word.

The elephant is **huge.**

Big is a synonym of *huge.*

The elephant is **big.**

Practice It! Read these words. Write the words that are synonyms next to each other.

small   **quick**   **fast**   **little**

Fluency

Rate When you read, try to read the sentences as if you are talking. Think about what the sentences mean.

Practice It!

1. Tom can get the hats from Mom.

2. Use a box to pack the blue hats.

3. Pop can help get a box of wigs.

Common Core State Standards
Language 5.c. Identify real-life connections between words and their use (e.g., note places at home that are *cozy*).
Also Speaking/Listening 1.

Let's Talk About

Read Together

Wild Animals

- Share information about wild animals.

- Discuss how wild animals take care of their babies.

READING STREET ONLINE
CONCEPT TALK VIDEO
www.ReadingStreet.com

Common Core State Standards
Foundational Skills 2. Demonstrate understanding of spoken words, syllables, and sounds (phonemes). **Also Foundational Skills 2.c., Speaking/Listening 6.**

Phonemic Awareness

Let's Listen for

Sounds

- Find five people who are doing something. Tell what they are doing.

- Find two actions that rhyme with *ends*. Say the sounds in each word.

- Find two actions that rhyme with *pumping*. Say the sounds in each word.

Read Together

READING STREET ONLINE
SOUND-SPELLING CARDS
www.ReadingStreet.com

Common Core State Standards
Foundational Skills 3.f. Read words with
inflectional endings.
Also Foundational Skills 3., 3.b., 3.g.

Envision It! Sounds to Know

pulls

ending -s

READING STREET ONLINE
SOUND-SPELLING CARDS
www.ReadingStreet.com

Phonics

Inflected Ending -s

Words I Can Blend

s	i	t	s
a	d	d	s
t	a	g	s

g	r	i	n	s

c	l	a	p	s

Sentences I Can Read

1. Lin sits and adds as Pat
tags Jill.

2. Kim grins and claps.

Words I Can Read

eat

four

five

her

this

too

Sentences I Can Read

1. Four kids eat yams, and Jan snacks on five ham bits too.

2. This is a big hat that fits her.

Common Core State Standards
Foundational Skills 3.f. Read words with inflectional endings.
Also Foundational Skills 3., 3.g.

Envision It! | **Sounds to Know**

drinking

ending -ing

READING STREET ONLINE
SOUND-SPELLING CARDS
www.ReadingStreet.com

Phonics

🎯 Inflected Ending *-ing*

Words I Can Blend

p a ck i ng

c a m p i ng

m i s s i ng

h a n d i ng

s p i l l i ng

Sentences I Can Read

1. Mack is packing for his camping trip and missing Mom.

2. Will is handing his glass to Sam and spilling his milk.

Fran has a list. Fran fills it with five jobs. Fran has to eat. Doll has to eat too. That is two jobs.

Fran sits and adds. That is three jobs.

Fran is filling her pack. That is four jobs.

Fran naps. This is her last job.
Fran is passing the list to Jan.

You've learned

- Inflected Ending -s
- Inflected Ending -ing

High-Frequency Words

eat	four	five
her	this	too

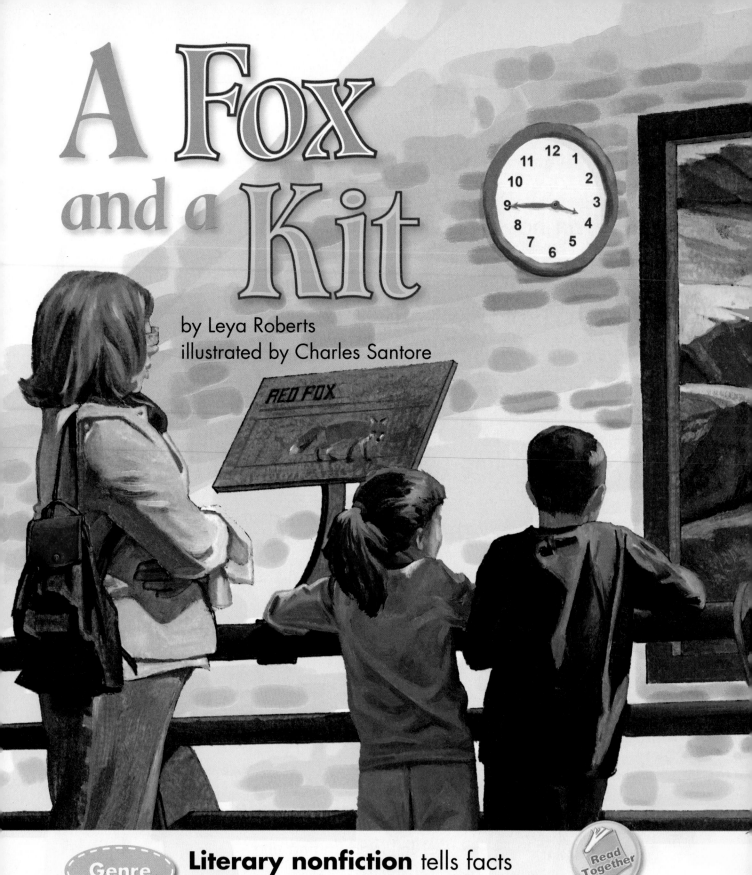

A Fox and a Kit

by Leya Roberts
illustrated by Charles Santore

RED FOX

Genre **Literary nonfiction** tells facts about the real world. It is sometimes told like a story. You will read about a fox and her kit at the zoo.

Question of the Week

How do wild animals take care of their babies?

It is four.
This fox naps on the rocks.
Her kit naps on the rocks too.

The kit sits up.
His mom sits up.

It is five.
This man is fixing dinner.
The kit and his mom will eat.

The kit is licking his lips.
His mom is licking her lips.

The kit is playing.
His mom is playing.
The kit nips and tags his mom.

The kit is on the rocks.
His mom will get him.
She picks him up and takes him back.

The kit spots his mom.
His mom spots him.

We like to watch this kit and
his mom!
We can watch lots of animals.

Common Core State Standards
Informational Text 2. Identify the main
topic and retell key details of a text.
Also Informational Text 1., Writing 2.

Envision It! Retell

Think Critically

1. *A Fox and a Kit* is about a mother fox and her kit. Tell about how another animal mother takes care of her baby. Text to World

2. What does the author want you to learn by reading this selection? Author's Purpose

3. What is the selection mostly about? Main Idea and Details

4. What did you learn about foxes by reading this selection? Important Ideas

5. **Look Back and Write** Look back at page 109. Write about how the fox takes care of her kit. Use evidence from the selection.

Key Ideas and Details • Text Evidence

Charles Santore

Charles Santore went to a zoo to learn about foxes. Mr. Santore also put pictures of foxes all around his studio to help him paint the pictures he needed for this story. Animals are a big part of his work.

Here are other books illustrated by Charles Santore.

Use the Reading Log in the *Reader's and Writer's Notebook* to record your independent reading.

113

Common Core State Standards
Writing 3. Write narratives in which they recount two or more appropriately sequenced events, include some details regarding what happened, use temporal words to signal event order, and provide some sense of closure.
Also Language 1.j., 2.b.

Let's Write It!

Read Together

Key Features of a Personal Narrative

- tells a story about a real event in the author's life
- tells how the author feels about it

READING STREET ONLINE
GRAMMAR JAMMER
www.ReadingStreet.com

Personal Narrative

A **personal narrative** tells of an event in the author's life. The student model on the next page is an example of a personal narrative.

Writing Prompt Think about a time you watched some animals. Write a narrative about it.

Writer's Checklist

Remember, you should . . .

✓ write about a time when you saw an animal or animals.

✓ use words that tell how you felt about what happened.

✓ write sentences that tell about the event from the beginning to the end.

The Ducks

Once I saw two ducks.

They swam in the pond.

They ate plants.

I wanted to swim!

I like to see ducks.

**Writing Trait
Voice**
Your writing tells how you feel. This writer shows feelings.

Genre
This **personal narrative** tells about an event that happened in the writer's own life.

A **declarative sentence** begins with a capital letter and ends with a period.

Conventions

- ### Declarative Sentences
  Remember A **declarative sentence** is a telling sentence.
- It begins with a capital letter and ends with a period.

Genre
Fable

- A fable is a short story that teaches a lesson, or moral.

- The characters in a fable are often animals that speak and act like people.

- The author wants readers to connect a fable's moral to their personal experiences.

- Read "The Fox and the Grapes." Look for elements that make this story a fable.

Read Together

The Fox and the Grapes

adapted from Aesop

One day, a fox wanted grapes.

But he could not reach them.

The fox tried again and again.

116

At last, the fox gave up.

"I did not want those sour grapes anyway," he said.

Moral: It is easy to dislike what you cannot get.

Let's Think About...

How do you know this story is a fable? **Fable**

Let's Think About...

What does the moral of the fable mean? How can you connect the meaning to things that have happened to you? **Fable**

Let's Think About...

Reading Across Texts How are the foxes in *A Fox and a Kit* and "The Fox and the Grapes" alike? How are they different?

Writing Across Texts Imagine the foxes in *A Fox and a Kit* could talk to the fox in "The Fox and the Grapes." Write what they would say to him. Write what he would say to them.

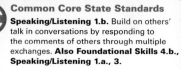

Common Core State Standards

Speaking/Listening 1.b. Build on others' talk in conversations by responding to the comments of others through multiple exchanges. **Also Foundational Skills 4.b., Speaking/Listening 1.a., 3.**

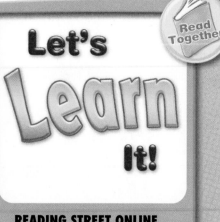

Let's Learn It!

Read Together

READING STREET ONLINE
VOCABULARY ACTIVITIES
www.ReadingStreet.com

Get Ready For Grade 2

Stay on topic when you speak.

Listening and Speaking

Share Information and Ideas When we share ideas with others, we speak clearly. We listen carefully to other ideas. We ask questions if we need more information.

Practice It! Discuss your favorite animal. Speak clearly in sentences. Stay on topic during the discussion. Listen carefully, take notes, and ask questions if you do not understand something.

Vocabulary

When we put words in **alphabetical order,** we look at the first letter in each word. Then we think about the alphabet and remember which letter comes first. If two words start with the same letter, we look at the second letter.

Practice It! Read these words. Write them in alphabetical order.

dog　　　**sit**　　　**tan**　　　**step**

Fluency

Rate When you read, try to read the sentences as if you were talking. Don't read too quickly or too slowly.

Practice It!

1. Tim can help by packing this bag.

2. The cat eats and naps.

3. The fox naps too.

Common Core State Standards
Speaking/Listening 1. Participate in collaborative conversations with diverse partners about grade 1 topics and texts with peers and adults in small and larger groups.
Also Language 5.c.

Oral Vocabulary

Let's Talk About

Read Together

Wild Animals

- Take part in a discussion about wild animals that live in our neighborhood.
- Share ideas about the habitats of wild animals that live in our neighborhood.

READING STREET ONLINE
CONCEPT TALK VIDEO
www.ReadingStreet.com

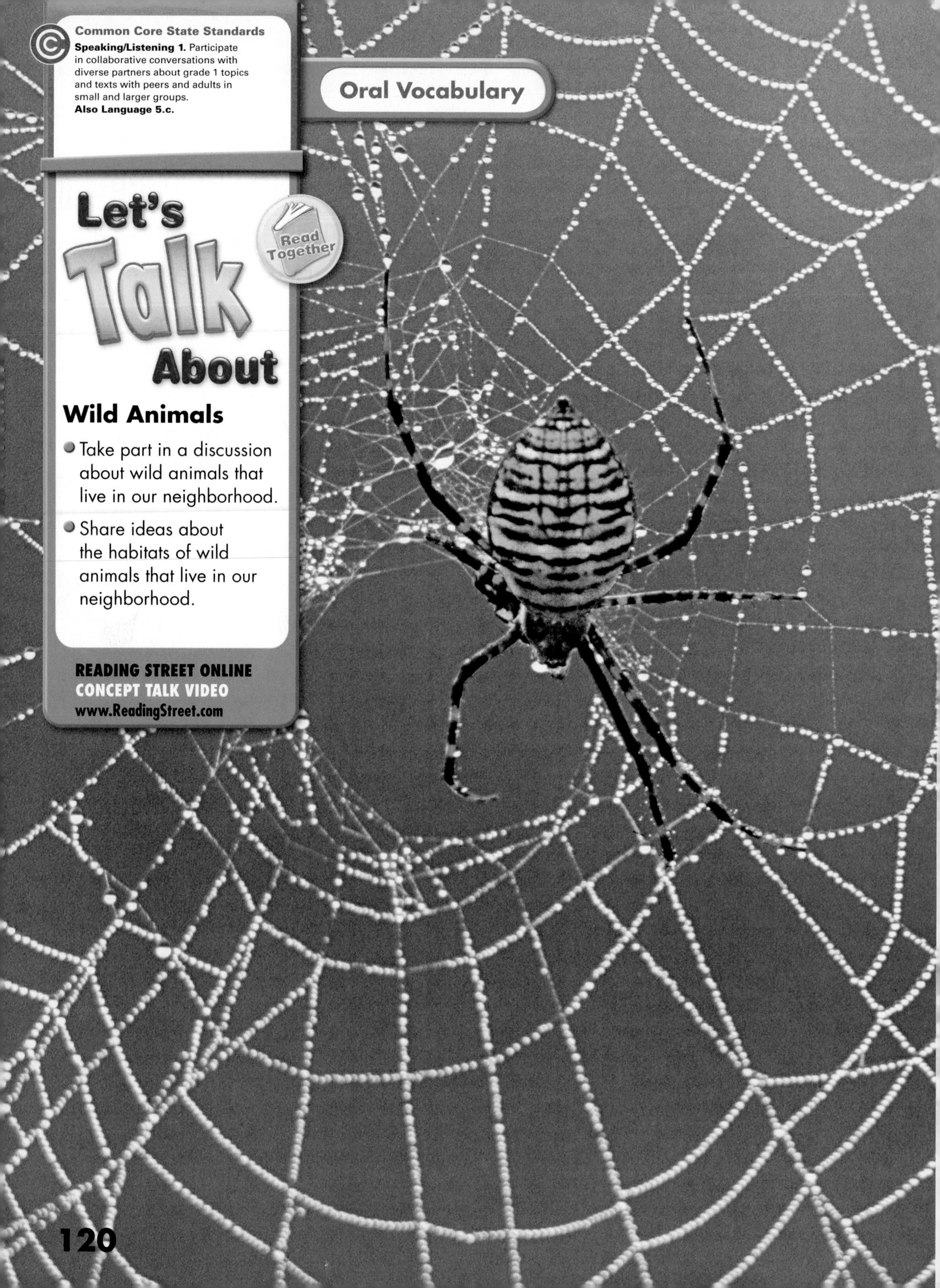

121

Common Core State Standards
Foundational Skills 2.c. Isolate and pronounce initial, medial vowel, and final sounds (phonemes) in spoken single-syllable words. **Also Foundational Skills 2.b., 2.d.**

Let's Listen for

Sounds

Read Together

- Find three things that rhyme with *tack*.

- Find five things that contain the short *e* sound. Say each word.

- Find something that rhymes with *best*. Say each sound in that word.

- Find something that starts with the sounds /spr/.

READING STREET ONLINE
SOUND-SPELLING CARDS
www.ReadingStreet.com

Common Core State Standards
Foundational Skills 3. Know and apply grade-level phonics and word analysis skills in decoding words.
Also Foundational Skills 3.g.

Envision It! | **Sounds to Know**

elephant

short e

READING STREET ONLINE
SOUND-SPELLING CARDS
www.ReadingStreet.com

Phonics

Short *e: e*

Words I Can Blend

B	e	n
g	e	t
p	e	t
m	e	s	s
t	e	l	l

Sentences I Can Read

1. Ben can get a pet.

2. Tell him to fix his mess.

Words I Can Read

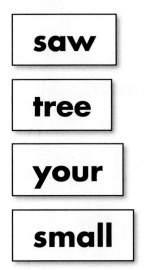

saw

tree

your

small

Sentences I Can Read

1. Nell saw a big nest in the tree.

2. A small pen is on your desk.

Common Core State Standards
Foundational Skills 3. Know and apply grade-level phonics and word analysis skills in decoding words.
Also Foundational Skills 3.a., 3.g.

Envision It! | Sounds to Know

train

consonant blend

READING STREET ONLINE
SOUND-SPELLING CARDS
www.ReadingStreet.com

Phonics

🔊 Initial Consonant Blends

Words I Can Blend

s	t	o	p	
b	l	a	ck	
p	l	a	n	s
s	t	e	p	
g	r	a	s	s

Sentences I Can Read

1. Sam will stop and get his black vest.

2. Ned plans to step on grass.

Deb and Spot stop at a small tree.
Drip! Drip! Drip! Deb gets wet.

Deb saw Spot. Spot gets wet.
Deb! Your dress is wet.
"What is it?" asks Deb.

Deb spots a nest. The mom in the nest
lets her kids sip drips from a wet stem.

The drips get Deb and Spot wet.

You've learned

◉ Short e: e
◉ Initial Consonant Blends

High-Frequency Words

saw   tree
your   small

Get the Egg!

by Alyssa Satin Capucilli

illustrated by Bernard Adnet

Genre

Realistic fiction is a made-up story that could really happen. In the next story you will read about a boy and a girl like you.

Question of the Week

Which wild animals live in our neighborhood?

Kim saw Brad at the tree.
A big red bird is in its nest, Kim.

Yes, Brad.
Six eggs sit in the nest.

Snap! A big twig hit the nest!
Snap, snap!
The big twig hit an egg!

Stop the egg, Brad. Stop it!
Can you get it?

The net! Get your net, Brad.
You can help.
Get the egg in your net.

Yes! You did it, Brad.
You can help, Kim.
Set the egg back in its nest.

Brad is at the tree.
The big red bird is back, Kim.

Yes, Brad.
It is in its nest.
Six small birds sit in the nest!

Common Core State Standards

Literature 2. Retell stories, including key details, and demonstrate understanding of their central message or lesson. **Also Literature 1., Writing 5.**

Envision It! | Retell

READING STREET ONLINE
STORY SORT
www.ReadingStreet.com

Think Critically

1. In *Get the Egg!*, Brad and Kim have an adventure. Find and read one part of the story that reminds you of something exciting that has happened to you. Text to Self

2. Why did the author write this story? Author's Purpose

3. What is this story about?

   Main Idea and Details

4. Does this story have a happy ending? Explain.

   Story Structure

5. **Look Back and Write** Look back at pages 134 and 135. Write about how Brad and Kim save the red bird's egg. Provide evidence from the story. Discuss what you wrote with a partner.

Key Ideas and Details • Text Evidence

Alyssa Satin Capucilli

Alyssa Satin Capucilli writes stories in a notebook she calls her "treasure keeper." Ms. Capucilli once saved a bird that had fallen from its nest. She wrote *Get the Egg!* when she remembered how proud she felt after saving the bird.

Here are other books by Alyssa Satin Capucilli.

Use the Reading Log in the *Reader's and Writer's Notebook* to record your independent reading.

139

Common Core State Standards

Writing 3. Write narratives in which they recount two or more appropriately sequenced events, include some details regarding what happened, use temporal words to signal event order, and provide some sense of closure. **Also Writing 5., Language 1.j.**

Let's Write It!

Read Together

Key Features of a Realistic Story

- characters, events, and setting seem real
- characters do things that really can happen

READING STREET ONLINE
GRAMMAR JAMMER
www.ReadingStreet.com

Realistic Story

A **realistic story** is a made-up story that could happen in real life. The student model on the next page is an example of a realistic story.

Writing Prompt Think about animals in neighborhoods. Write a realistic story about two friends seeing an animal.

Writer's Checklist

Remember, you should . . .

☑ write a story with events that could really happen.

☑ make sure your story has a beginning, a middle, and an end.

☑ make sure any question ends with a question mark.

The Deer

A deer came to the park.
Then Zef and Teresa saw it.
The deer looked hungry.
Zef wanted to leave it six
grapes. His dad said no. Will
they see the deer again?

Genre
Realistic Story
This story tells about an event that could really happen.

Writing Trait
Organization
The story has a beginning, middle, and end.

This **question** begins with a capital letter and ends with a question mark.

Conventions

- **Interrogative Sentences**

  Remember A **question** asks something. It begins with a **capital letter.** It ends with a **question mark (?).**

Common Core State Standards
Informational Text 6. Distinguish between information provided by pictures or other illustrations and information provided by the words in a text. **Also Informational Text 3.**

Genre
How-to Article

Read Together

- A how-to article is procedural text that tells you how to make or do something.

- A how-to article is usually a set of directions.

- The directions in a how-to article are often numbered. They are listed in the order you should do each step, from first to last.

- If you follow the directions as they are written, you will be successful.

- Read "Help the Birds." As you read, think about what you've learned about how-to articles.

Help the Birds

Birds like to eat.
You can help.

1 Get a small twig.

2 Dip it here.

Peanut Butter

3 Dip it in this.

Bird Seed

4 Clip it to your tree.
Watch the birds come.

Let's **Think** About...

What might happen if you did not follow the second step?
How-to Article

Let's **Think** About...

Read the directions, following each step. What did you make or do?
How-to Article

Let's **Think** About...

Reading Across Texts How is the girl in "Help the Birds" like Brad and Kim in *Get the Egg!*?

Writing Across Texts If Brad and Kim decided to make treats for the six small birds, what would they make? Write a how-to article for them.

Common Core State Standards
Speaking/Listening 4. Describe people, places, things, and events with relevant details, expressing ideas and feelings clearly. **Also Foundational Skills 4.b., Language 5.b.**

Let's **Learn** It!

Read Together

READING STREET ONLINE
VOCABULARY ACTIVITIES
www.ReadingStreet.com

Today was a fun day! We went to a huge park. We played all day. We saw two little rabbits by two tall, green trees.

Get Ready For Grade 2

Use descriptive words to make stories more interesting.

Listening and Speaking

Give Descriptions We can use descriptive words, or adjectives, to make a story we tell more interesting. Words such as *fun* and *tall* tell about people, places, things, and events.

Practice It! Tell others about something that happened to you. Use descriptive words, such as *green* and *tall,* to make the story more interesting.

Vocabulary

When we **sort words,** we put them into groups that make sense.

cat dog

raccoon squirrel

These animals are tame.   **These animals are wild.**

Practice It! Read these words. Sort them into two groups—animals that fly and animals that do not fly.

fox   ox   bee   cow   bird

Fluency

Appropriate Phrasing When you come to a period, you know it is the end of a sentence. Stop reading at the period.

Practice It!

1. Stop and get your net.

2. Ben, come see the frog by the tree.

Common Core State Standards

Speaking/Listening 4. Describe people, places, things, and events with relevant details, expressing ideas and feelings clearly.

Let's Talk About

Read Together

Wild Animals

- Share information about wild animals from all around the world.

- Discuss what we can learn about animals by watching them.

READING STREET ONLINE
CONCEPT TALK VIDEO
www.ReadingStreet.com

Common Core State Standards
Foundational Skills 2.c. Isolate and pronounce initial, medial vowel, and final sounds (phonemes) in spoken single-syllable words. **Also Foundational Skills 2.b.**

Let's Listen for

Sounds

- Find two things that rhyme with *trust*.
- Find five things that contain the short *u* sound.
- Find something that rhymes with *dunk*. Say each sound in the word.

READING STREET ONLINE
SOUND-SPELLING CARDS
www.ReadingStreet.com

Read Together

Common Core State Standards
Foundational Skills 3. Know and apply grade-level phonics and word analysis skills in decoding words.
Also Foundational Skills 3.g.

Envision It! Sounds to Know

umbrella

short u

READING STREET ONLINE
SOUND-SPELLING CARDS
www.ReadingStreet.com

Phonics

Short *u: u*

Words I Can Blend

f u n

s t u f f

c l u b

t r u ck

t u g

Sentences I Can Read

1. Ken gets fun stuff in his club.

2. My big truck can tug his little truck.

Words I Can Read

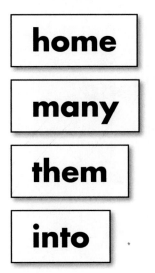

Sentences I Can Read

1. Fred has many rugs at home.

2. Tuck them into bed.

Envision It! | Sounds to Know

lamp

consonant blend

READING STREET ONLINE
SOUND-SPELLING CARDS
www.ReadingStreet.com

Phonics

Final Consonant Blends

Words I Can Blend

j u s t

d e s k

b e s t

t e n t

s a n d

Sentences I Can Read

1. Jess just sat at his desk.

2. Bud set up his best tent on hot sand.

I Can Read!

Judd has fun in mud. Will Judd jump in mud? Yes!

And Judd will stand on the rug. Many clumps of mud end up on the rug!

Mom and Dad get home. "Yuck! Get into the tub, Judd."

Judd gets rid of his mud in the tub. Mom and Dad are glad. Judd can help them rub mud from the rug.

You've learned

🔄 Short *u: u*
🔄 Final Consonant Blends

High-Frequency Words
home   many   them   into

Animal Park

by Judy Nayer

Genre **Literary nonfiction** is about real places and events told like a story. Next you will read about some wild animals in Africa.

Africa

Question of the Week

What can we learn about wild animals by watching them?

155

The hot sun is up at camp.
Camp is in a big, big park.

This land is home to many
animals. Can we see them?
Yes! Just get in the truck.

Bump, bump, bump!
Quick, stop!
A band of zebras runs past us.
They blend into the grass.

Big cats rest up.
They had a big hunt.
Cubs can bat at bugs.

Big birds stand in tan grass.
They can run fast!

Big hippos sit in wet mud.
It is hot, but mud is not hot!

Big elephants stand and sip
in the pond.
They can stomp and swim in it.

Bump, bump, bump!
The truck is back at camp.

This park is home to many animals.
It was fun to see them!

Common Core State Standards
Informational Text 1. Ask and answer
questions about key details in a text.
Also Informational Text 2., Writing 5.

Envision It! | Retell

Think Critically

Read Together

1. Put yourself in the animal park. Read the part of the selection that tells about the animals you would like to see. Text to Self

2. Does the author seem to like animals? Explain why or why not. Author's Purpose

3. Why do hippos sit in the mud? Cause and Effect

4. Which animals does the author see before the hippos? Text Structure

5. **Look Back and Write** Look back at the photographs in the selection. Choose an animal that was in the big park. Use facts from the selection to write about the animal you choose.

Key Ideas and Details • Text Evidence

Judy Nayer

Maybe you have seen big animals in a zoo. Judy Nayer wanted to show you where some of these animals really live, in Africa. Ms. Nayer writes every day. She says, "I often work late at night, when it's very quiet."

Here are other books by Judy Nayer.

Use the Reading Log in the *Reader's and Writer's Notebook* to record your independent reading.

165

Common Core State Standards

Writing 2. Write informative/explanatory texts in which they name a topic, supply some facts about the topic, and provide some sense of closure. **Also Language 1.j.**

Let's Write It!

Read Together

Key Features of a Brief Composition

- tells about real people or things
- tells about just one topic

READING STREET ONLINE
GRAMMAR JAMMER
www.ReadingStreet.com

Brief Composition

Compositions tell about real things. The student model on the next page is an example of a brief composition.

Writing Prompt Think about wild animals. Write a composition about what people learn by watching wild animals.

Writer's Checklist

Remember, you should ...

☑ tell about real wild animals.

☑ make sure each sentence tells one idea.

☑ write an exclamatory sentence at the end, and say the sentence with strong feeling.

Watching Birds

Mom and I see birds in the trees. They are not pets. We learn about birds. Birds eat berries. They live in nests. Birds eat a lot!

Writing Trait Focus
Sentences should **focus** on the topic.

Genre Brief Composition
This article tells facts about real birds.

This **exclamatory sentence** shows that the writer is surprised.

Conventions

- **Exclamatory Sentences**

  Remember An **exclamatory sentence** shows a strong feeling. It ends with an **exclamation mark (!).**

Common Core State Standards
Literature 10. With prompting and support, read prose and poetry of appropriate complexity for grade 1.

Genre
Poetry

- *Poetry* is another word for *poems*. The author of a poem is called a poet.

- A poem tells a story or expresses the poet's feelings about something.

- A poem is written in lines. Often the words at the ends of the lines rhyme.

- A poem usually has a rhythm, or a regular pattern of beats.

- Some poems have alliteration, or words close to each other with the same beginning sound.

- As you read "My Dog Rags," "Raccoon," and "The Hippo," look for elements of poetry.

- Find the alliteration in "My Dog Rags." Which words begin with the same sound?

My Dog Rags

I have a dog and his
name is Rags.

He eats so much that
his tummy sags.

His ears flip-flop
and his tail wig-wags,

And when he walks
he zig-zig-zags!

Raccoon *by Betsy Lewin*

Raccoons are not a fussy clan
when it comes time to eat.

They'll even raid a garbage can
to find a midnight treat.

The Hippo *by Douglas Florian*

By day the hippo loves to float

On swamps and lakes,
much like a boat.

At night from water it retreats,

And eats

and eats

and eats

and eats.

illustrated by Patrice Aggs

Let's **Think** About...

Point out the words that rhyme in each poem. Clap the rhythm in each poem. **Poetry**

Let's **Think** About...

Reading Across Texts How are the animals in *Animal Park* and the animals in the poems alike? How are they different?

Writing Across Texts Choose any animal, except the hippo, in *Animal Park*. Write a two-line poem about the animal. Use rhythm and words that rhyme at the ends of the lines.

Common Core State Standards
Speaking/Listening 4. Describe people, places, things, and events with relevant details, expressing ideas and feelings clearly. **Also Foundational Skills 4.b.**

First, I write the letter. Then I put it in the envelope. After I write the address on the envelope, I add a stamp. Then I...

Let's **Learn** It!

Read Together

READING STREET ONLINE
VOCABULARY ACTIVITIES
www.ReadingStreet.com

Listening and Speaking

Get Ready For Grade 2

Be a good listener when you follow directions.

Follow, Restate, Give Directions When we follow directions, we use good listening skills. We ask the speaker questions. We repeat the directions to show we understand.

Practice It! Listen to your teacher's directions on how to mail a letter. Restate the directions. Then give new directions to a partner. Use sentences.

170

Vocabulary

An **antonym** is a word that means the opposite of another word.

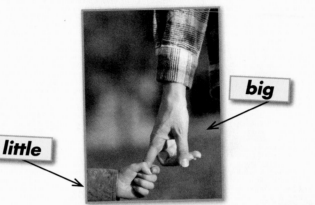

big

little

Practice It! Read these words. Write and say an antonym for each word.

fast   in   up   on   back

Fluency

Appropriate Phrasing When you come to a question mark as you read, make your voice go up as if you are asking a question.

Practice It!

1. Can Gus put his frogs into the pond?

2. Where will Bud go to swim?

3. Will the dog run with them at last?

Pets

cat

gerbil

kitten

guinea pig

turtle

hamster

parakeet

goldfish

puppy

dog

iguana

rabbit

173

Farm Animals

chick

hen

rooster

horse

goat

pig

cow

ox

calf

pony

sheep

175

Forest Animals

chipmunk

raccoon

turkey

skunk

opossum

bear

beaver

deer

squirrel

porcupine

Desert Animals

jack rabbit

road runner

tarantula

armadillo

iguana

rattlesnake

camel

coyote

Grassland Animals

cheetah

hyena

rhinoceros

giraffe

anteater

lion

hippopotamus

elephant

zebra

178

Water Animals

frog

lobster

octopus

clam

fish

jellyfish

shark

alligator

dolphin

manatee

whale

179

Cold-Climate Animals

penguin

lemming

walrus

seal

polar bear

arctic fox

moose
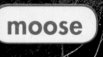

arctic wolf

Underground Animals

mole

meerkat

badger

prairie dog

earthworm

trapdoor spider

181

Birds

woodpecker

ostrich

goose

robin

crow

cardinal

eagle

duck

owl

hummingbird

pigeon

seagull

Insects and Bugs

ant

caterpillar

beetle

ladybug

cricket

butterfly

fly

lightning bug

spider

grasshopper

bee

183

Sam, Come Back!

come
in
my
on
way

The Big Blue Ox

blue
from
get
help
little
use

Pig in a Wig

she
take
up
what

A Fox and a Kit

eat
five
four
her
this
too

Animal Park

home
into
many
them

Get the Egg!

saw
small
tree
your

Aa Bb Cc

Dd Ee Ff

Gg Hh Ii

Jj Kk Ll

Mm Nn Oo

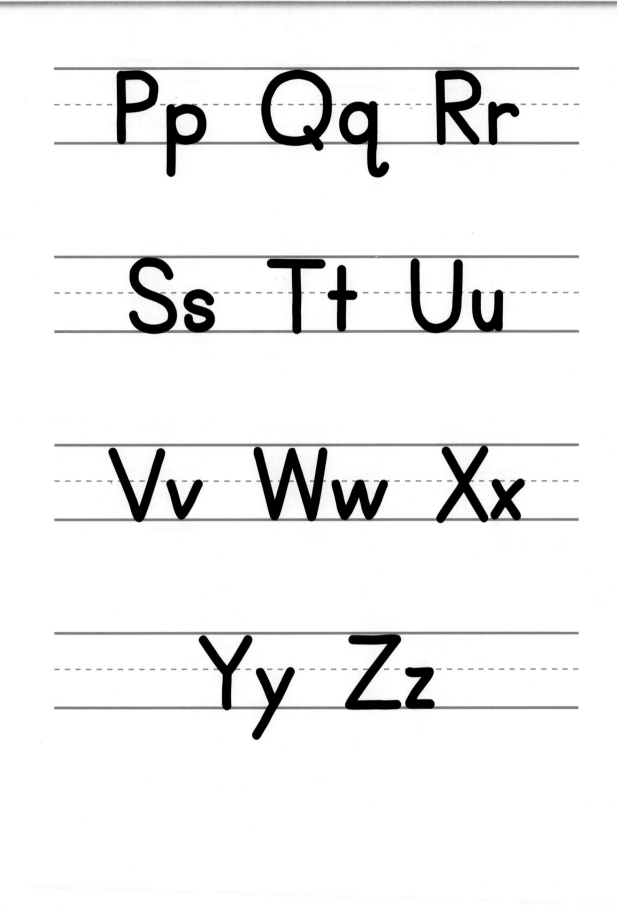

P p Q q R r

S s T t U u

V v W w X x

Y y Z z

Acknowledgments

Text

Grateful acknowledgment is made to the following for copyrighted material:

Henry Holt and Company, LLC.

"Raccoon" from *Animal Snackers* by Betsy Lewin. Copyright © 1980, 2004 by Betsy Lewin. Used by arrangement with Henry Holt and Company, LLC.

Houghton Mifflin Harcourt Publishing Company

"The Hippo" from *Mammalabilia: Poems and Paintings* by Douglas Florian. Copyright © 2000 by Douglas Florian. Reproduced by permission of Houghton Mifflin Harcourt Publishing Company. All rights reserved.

Note: Every effort has been made to locate the copyright owner of material reproduced on this component. Omissions brought to our attention will be corrected in subsequent editions.

Cover: (B) ©Theo Allots/Getty Images, (T) Getty Images

Illustrations

EI2–EI5 Mary Anne Lloyd

EI8–EI17 Chris Lensch

14 Robbie Short

20-29, 46, 48, 50–56, 74-83 Janet Stevens

34, 35 Maribel Suarez

40 Marilyn Janovitz

62, 63 Lindsey Gardiner

68 Paul Meisel

98 Ariel Pang

102-111 Charles Santore

116, 117 Steve Mack

126 Carol Koeller

128-141 Bernard Adnet

154 Victor Rivas

Photographs

Every effort has been made to secure permission and provide appropriate credit for photographic material. The publisher deeply regrets any omission and pledges to correct errors called to its attention in subsequent editions.

Unless otherwise acknowledged, all photographs are the property of Pearson Education, Inc.

Photo locators denoted as follows: Top (T), Center (C), Bottom (B), Left (L), Right (R), Background (Bkgd)

4 (T) ©LarryWilliams/Corbis

10 (B) ©LarryWilliams/Corbis

12 (T) ©Royalty-Free/Corbis, (B) Frank Siteman/Stock Boston

16 GRIN/NASA

36 ©DK Images

38 ©Picture Partners/Alamy Images

39 (TL) Kaz Chiba/Getty Images, (B) LWA-JDC/Corbis, (CR) The York Dispatch, Jason Plotkin/AP/Wide World Photos

42 ©Premaphotos/Nature Picture Library

44 ©Asgeir Helgestad/Nature Picture Library

65 Getty Images, Joe McDonald/Corbis, Peter Arnold/Getty Images

66 (B) ©Chris Marona/Photo Researchers, Inc.

67 (B) ©Royalty-Free/Corbis, (C) Alan Oddie/PhotoEdit

70 ©Vittorio Bruno/ Shutterstock

72 ©Brian Stablyk/Getty Images, ©DLILLC/Corbis

88 (BL) Getty Images

89 (TL) Mark Richards/PhotoEdit

90 (BR) Peter Olive/Photofusion Picture Library/Alamy Images

91 (TR) A. Ramey/PhotoEdit, (TL) Bryan and Cherry Alexander/ ©Arcticphoto/ Alamy Images, (C) Dallas and John Heaton/Corbis

93 Daryl Balfour/Getty Images

94 (B) ©San Diego Zoo/Handout/Reuters/Corbis, (T) Weimann, Peter/Animals Animals/Earth Scenes

95 (BC) Gallo Images/Corbis, (BR) Karl Ammann/Corbis

98 ©JoeFoxDublin/Alamy Images

100 ©Andrea Matone/Alamy Images

118 (TR) Getty Images

120 Niall Benvie/Corbis

121 ©Aristide Economopoulos/Star Ledger/Corbis, (T) Dennis Avon/ Ardea, (BL) Jean Paul Ferrero/Ardea

124 Carleton Chinner/Shutterstock

126 ©Robert McGouey/Alamy Images

145 American Images Inc./Getty Images, Frank Lukasseck/Getty Images, Joel Sartore/Getty Images, Purestock/Getty Images

146 ©Frans Lanting/Corbis

147 (T) ©John Cancalosi/Alamy Images, (B) Steve Bower/Shutterstock

154 (TL) Getty Images, (Bkgd) Tim Davis/Corbis

156 (BR) Craig Lovell/Corbis, (Bkgd) Photo Researchers, Inc.

157 (TR) Corbis, (BR) Digital Stock, (CR) Digital Vision, (L) Staffan Widstrand/Corbis

158 (TC) Jupiter Images, (Bkgd) Tom Nebbia/Corbis

159 (CC) Art Wolfe/Art Wolfe Inc., (TC) Tom Brakefield/Corbis

160 (TC) Beverly Joubert/NGS Image Collection, (BC) Peter Johnson/ Corbis

161 ©Michele Burgess/Index Stock Imagery

162 (T) ©Theo Allofs/Getty Images

163 (TL) Brand X Pictures, (BL) David Young-Wolff/Alamy Images, (Bkgd) Digital Vision, (CL) Norbert Rosing/NGS Image Collection

165 (BL) Staffan Widstrand/Corbis

171 Mira/Alamy Images, Phil Schermeister /Getty Images

172 (TR) ©Jane Burton/DK Images, (CL) ©Karl Shone/DK Images, (TL) ©Marc Henrie/DK Images, (CR, BR) ©Paul Bricknell/DK Images, (CC) ©Richard Kolar/Animals Animals/Earth Scenes, (B) Getty Images

173 (T) DK Images, (BR, BL) Ingram Publishing

174 (BL) ©Dave King/DK Images, (TR) ©Gordon Clayton/DK Images, (TC) ©Mike Dunning/DK Images, (CR) Dave King/©DK Images, (BR) DK Images, (TL) Jane Burton/©DK Images

175 (BL) ©Bob Langrish/DK Images, (T, CR, BR) ©Gordon Clayton/ DK Images, (CL) ©Ike Geib/Grant Heilman Photography

176 (CC) ©Corbis Premium RF/Alamy, (CR) ©Dave King/ DK Images, (TCL) ©Dr. Harvey Barnett/Peter Arnold, Inc., (BR) ©G. K. & Vikki Hart/Getty Images, (TL) ©Gary W. Carter/Corbis, (BBC) ©S. J. Krasemann/Peter Arnold, Inc., (TC) ©W. Perry Conway/Corbis, (TR) Getty Images, (BL) Jane Burton/ ©DK Images, (BCL) Jupiter Images

177 (TL) ©Daniel Sweeney (escapeimages)/Alamy, (BR) ©imagebroker/Alamy, (BL) ©Philip Dowell/DK Images, (TC) ©Steve Hamblin/Alamy, (TCR) ©VStock/Index Open, (BCR) Dave King/DK Images, (TR) DK Images, (CL) Getty Images

178 (TCC) ©Ablestock/Alamy, (C) ©Dave King/DK Images, (CR) ©David Madison/Photoshot, (CL) ©Jim Zuckerman/Corbis, (TR) ©Juniors Bildarchiv/Alamy, (TL) ©Nature Picture Library/Alamy, (BL) ©Philip Dowell/DK Images, (TC) ©tony phelps/Alamy, (BR) DK Images

179 (TC) ©Colin Keates/DK Images, ©Comstock Images/Jupiter Images, (TR) ©Frank Greenaway/DK Images, (BL) ©Frank Staub/ PhotoLibrary Group, Inc., (BCC) ©Jim Stamates/Getty Images, (TCL) ©Kevin Moore/Alamy, (BCL) ©Lionel Isy-Schwart/Getty Images, (BCR) Digital Stock, (TL) DK Images, (TCR, C) Getty Images

180 (BL) ©Allen Thornton/Alamy, (BR) ©Corbis Premium RF/ Alamy, (TC) ©David Hosking/Alamy Images, (TL) ©Jan Martin Will/ Shutterstock, (TR) ©Nigel McCall/Alamy, (CR) ©Ralph Lee Hopkins/ Wilderland Images, (TCL, CR) Getty Images

181 (CL) ©Corbis Premium RF/Alamy, (TR) ©Emile Wessels/Alamy, (BL) ©Hans Christoph Kappel/Nature Picture Library, (BR) ©Stefan Sollfors/Alamy, (TL, C) Index Open

182 (TCL) ©Arthur Morris/Corbis, (CR) ©Bill Dyer/Photo Researchers, Inc., (BCR, BCC) ©Cyril Laubscher/ DK Images, (TCC) ©Darrell Gulin/Corbis, (BR) ©Dinodia/ OmniPhoto Communications, Inc., (BCL) ©Jeff Lepore/Photo Researchers, Inc., (BC) ©John Edwards/Getty Images, (BL) ©Ray Coleman/Photo Researchers, Inc., (TL) ©Roy Rainford/Robert Harding World Imagery, (TR) ©Tom McHugh/Photo Researchers, Inc., (TCC) Getty Images

183 (TR) ©Colin Keates/DK Images, (TC) ©Cyndy Black/Robert Harding World Imagery, (BR, BC) ©Frank Greenaway/DK Images, (TCL) ©Neil Fletcher/DK Images, (BL) ©Rudi Von Briel/PhotoEdit, (TCC) ©Simon D. Pollard/Photo Researchers, Inc., (BCL) DK Images, (BL) Getty Images, (TL) Jupiter Images, (BCC) Robert & Linda Mitchell

High-Frequency Words

Identify and read the high-frequency words that you learned in unit R and unit 1.

Unit R.1
a
green
I
see

Unit R.2
like
one
the
we

Unit R.3
do
look
was
yellow
you

Unit R.4
are
have
that
they
two

Unit R.5
he
is
three
to
with

Unit R.6
for
go
here
me
where

Unit 1.1
come
in
my
on
way

Unit 1.2
she
take
up
what

Unit 1.3
blue
from
get
help
little
use

Unit 1.4
eat
five
four

her
this
too

Unit 1.5
saw
small
tree
your

Unit 1.6
home
into
many
them

Unit 2.1
catch
good
no
put
said
want

Unit 2.2
be
could
horse
of
old
paper

Unit 2.3
live
out
people
who
work

Unit 2.4
down
inside
now
there
together

Unit 2.5
around
find
food
grow
under
water

Unit 2.6
also
family
new
other
some
their

High-Frequency Words

Unit 3.1
always
become
day
everything
nothing
stays
things

Unit 3.2
any
enough
ever
every
own
sure
were

Unit 3.3
away
car
friends
house
our
school
very

Unit 3.4
afraid
again
few
how
read
soon

Unit 3.5
done
know
push
visit
wait

Unit 3.6
before
does
good-bye
oh
right
won't

Unit 4.1
about
enjoy
give
surprise
worry
would

Unit 4.2
colors
draw
drew
great
over
show
sign

Unit 4.3
found
mouth

once
took
wild

Unit 4.4
above
eight
laugh
moon
touch

Unit 4.5
picture
remember
room
stood
thought

Unit 4.6
across
because
dance
only
opened
shoes
told

Unit 5.1
along
behind
eyes
never
pulling
toward

Unit 5.2
door
loved
should
wood

Unit 5.3
among
another
instead
none

Unit 5.4
against
goes
heavy
kinds
today

Unit 5.5
built
early
learn
science
through

Unit 5.6
answered
carry
different
poor